Meet the
NEW YORK
GIANTS

BY
ZACK BURGESS

NORWOOD HOUSE PRESS

CHICAGO, ILLINOIS

NORWOODHOUSE🏠PRESS

P.O. Box 316598 • Chicago, Illinois 60631
For more information about Norwood House Press please visit our website at
www.norwoodhousepress.com or call 866-565-2900.

Photo Credits:
All photos courtesy of Associated Press, except for the following: Black Book Archives (6, 7, 15, 22),
Philadelphia Chewing Gum Co. (10 top), Topps, Inc. (10 bottom, 11 middle & bottom, 23),
McDonald's Corp. (11 top), Sports Illustrated for Kids (18).

Cover Photo: Kathy Willens/Associated Press

The football memorabilia photographed for this book is part of the authors' collection. The collectibles used
for artistic background purposes in this series were manufactured by many different card companies—
including Bowman, Donruss, Fleer, Leaf, O-Pee-Chee, Pacific, Panini America, Philadelphia Chewing Gum,
Pinnacle, Pro Line, Pro Set, Score, Topps, and Upper Deck—as well as several food brands, including
Crane's, Hostess, Kellogg's, McDonald's and Post.

Designer: Ron Jaffe
Series Editors: Mike Kennedy and Mark Stewart
Project Management: Black Book Partners, LLC.
Editorial Production: Lisa Walsh

LIBRARY OF CONGRESS CATALOGING-IN-PUBLICATION DATA
Names: Burgess, Zack.
Title: Meet the New York Giants / by Zack Burgess.
Description: Chicago, Illinois : Norwood House Press, [2016] | Series: Big
    picture sports | Includes bibliographical references and index. |
    Audience: Grade: K to Grade 3.
Identifiers: LCCN 2015022467| ISBN 9781599537368 (Library Edition : alk.
    paper) | ISBN 9781603578394 (eBook)
Subjects: LCSH: New York Giants (Football team)--Miscellanea--Juvenile
    literature.
Classification: LCC GV956.N4 B86 2016 | DDC 796.332/64097471--dc23
LC record available at http://lccn.loc.gov/2015022467

288N—072016
Manufactured in the United States of America in North Mankato, Minnesota

CONTENTS

Words in **bold type** are defined on page 24.

The Giants celebrate a touchdown.

CALL ME A GIANT

Fans of the New York Giants call their team "Big Blue." Of course, the players aren't really giants. But they play like them when it matters most. The Giants have treated their fans to some of the greatest wins in National Football League (NFL) history.

The Giants won the NFL championship in 1927, 1934, 1938, and 1956. In 1986, they won the Super Bowl for the first time. The Giants have always relied on great defensive stars. Two of their best were **Emlen Tunnell** ● ——→ and Lawrence Taylor.

Many fans believe Lawrence Taylor was the best Giant ever.

Everyone has a good seat at the Giants' stadium.

BEST SEAT IN THE HOUSE

The Giants play in New Jersey at the Meadowlands Sports Complex. This has been the team's home since 1976. In 2010, the Giants moved into a new stadium in the same area. It was built just a few feet away from the old stadium.

SHOE BOX

The trading cards on these pages show some of the best Giants ever.

MEL HEIN

CENTER & LINEBACKER · 1931-1945

Mel is the only offensive lineman to win the NFL Most Valuable Player award. In 15 seasons, he never missed a play because of an injury.

FRANK GIFFORD

RUNNING BACK · 1952-1964

Frank could do anything on a football field. He was a star runner, receiver, passer, kicker, and defender.

PHIL SIMMS

QUARTERBACK · 1979-1993

Phil led the Giants to their first Super Bowl victory. He also made the **Pro Bowl** twice.

LAWRENCE TAYLOR

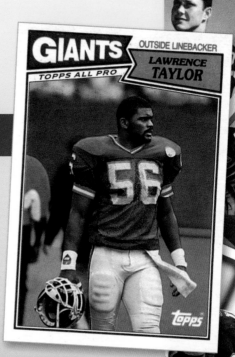

LINEBACKER · 1981-1993

Lawrence forced opponents to make a game plan just to stop him. He was named **All-Pro** eight times.

ODELL BECKHAM JR.

RECEIVER · FIRST YEAR WITH TEAM: 2014

Odell ran like a sprinter and could catch the ball with one hand. He scored 25 touchdowns in his first two seasons.

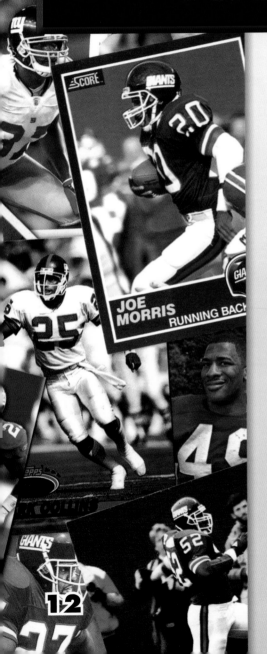

THE BIG PICTURE

Look at the two photos on page 13. Both appear to be the same. But they are not. There are three differences. Can you spot them?

Answers on page 23.

13

TRUE OR FALSE?

Eli Manning was a star quarterback. Two of these facts about him are **TRUE**. One is **FALSE**. Do you know which is which?

1 Eli holds the team record for most touchdown passes.

2 While playing in college at "Ole Miss," Eli tried to change his name to "Ole Manning."

3 Eli wrote a children's book called *Family Huddle* with his brother, Peyton.

Answer on page 23.

Eli Manning scans the field.

15

Victor Cruz greets young fans before a game.

Go Giants, Go!

Millions of Giants fans live within a few of hours of the team's stadium. They root for the Giants through thick and thin. Tickets for home games are almost impossible to get. They are often passed down from grandparents to parents to children!

ON THE MAP

Here is a look at where five Giants were born, along with a fun fact about each.

 1 **AMANI TOOMER · BERKELEY, CALIFORNIA**
Amani set the team record with 54 touchdown catches.

 2 **MICHAEL STRAHAN · HOUSTON, TEXAS**
Michael was voted into the **Hall of Fame** in 2014.

 3 **CHARLIE CONERLY · CLARKSDALE, TENNESSEE**
Charlie led the team to the 1956 NFL championship.

 4 **JASON PIERRE-PAUL · DEERFIELD BEACH, FLORIDA**
"JPP" was the first NFL player with a blocked field goal, fumble recovery, and **quarterback sack** in the same game.

 5 **RAUL ALLEGRE · TORREON, COAHUILA, MEXICO**
Raul's kicking helped the Giants win the Super Bowl in 1986.

MICHAEL STRAHAN
Defensive End · New York Giants

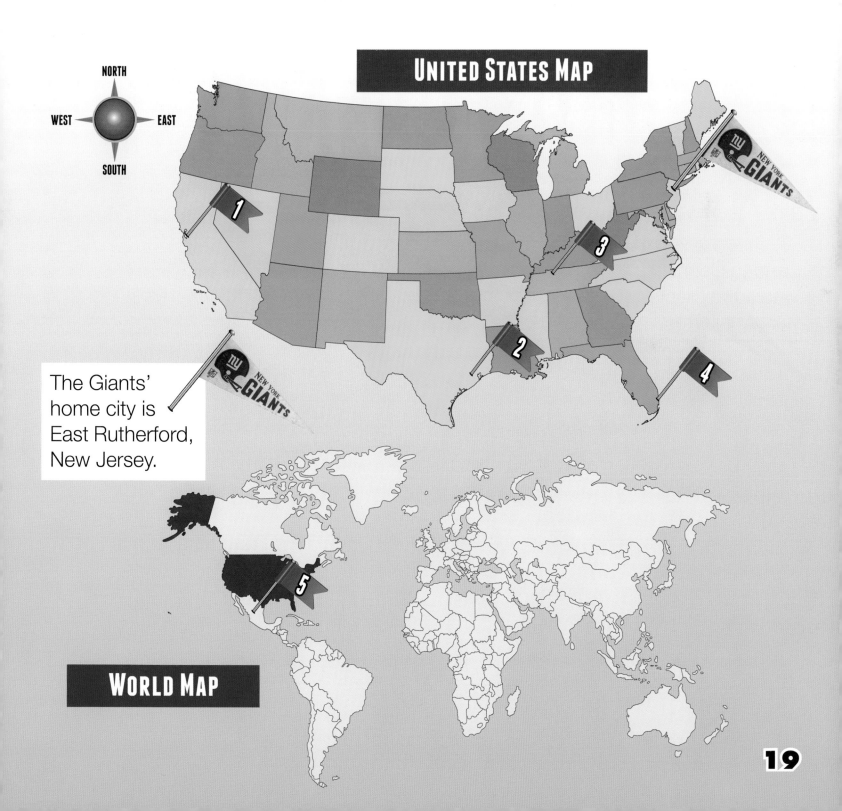

UNITED STATES MAP

NORTH

WEST ● EAST

SOUTH

NEW YORK GIANTS

1

3

2

4

The Giants' home city is East Rutherford, New Jersey.

NEW YORK GIANTS

5

WORLD MAP

HOME AND AWAY

Landon Collins wears the Giants' home uniform.

Football teams wear different uniforms for home and away games. The main colors of the Giants are blue, white, red, and gray.

Odell Beckham Jr. wears the Giants' away uniform.

The Giants' helmet is blue with a red stripe down the middle. It shows *ny* on each side. This stands for New York.

The Giants played in the Super Bowl five times from 1986 to 2011. They won the championship four times. Coach **Bill Parcells** led the team to its first two Super Bowl victories. Tom Coughlin coached the Giants to their next two.

RECORD BOOK

These Giants set team records.

Y. A. TITTLE
NEW YORK GIANTS · QUARTERBACK

TOUCHDOWN PASSES	RECORD
Season: **Y.A. Tittle** (1963)	36
Career: Eli Manning	294

RECEIVING YARDS	RECORD
Season: Victor Cruz (2011)	1,536
Career: Amani Toomer	9.497

RUSHING YARDS	RECORD
Season: Tiki Barber (2005)	1,860
Career: Tiki Barber	10,449

ANSWERS FOR THE BIG PICTURE
#77 changed to #73, #55's name changed to FREDDIE, and the stripes on #65's pants changed.

ANSWER FOR TRUE AND FALSE
#2 is false. Eli never tried to change his name.

Football Words

All-Pro
An honor given to the best NFL player at each position.

Hall of Fame
The museum in Canton, Ohio, where football's greatest players are honored.

Pro Bowl
The NFL's annual all-star game.

Quarterback Sack
A tackle of the quarterback that loses yardage.

Index

Photos are on **BOLD** numbered pages.

About the Author

Zack Burgess has been writing about sports for more than 20 years. He has lived all over the country and interviewed lots of All-Pro football players, including Brett Favre, Eddie George, Jerome Bettis, Shannon Sharpe, and Rich Gannon. Zack was the first African American beat writer to cover Major League Baseball when he worked for the *Kansas City Star*.

About the Giants

Learn more at these websites:

www.giants.com • www.profootballhof.com
www.teamspiritextras.com/Overtime/html/giants.html